Contents

INTODUCTION

The first of the iPad Air series was released in late 2013. It replaced the 4th generation model as the forerunner in its tablet lineup as the next generation 9.7 inch iPad. The first of the iPad Air took up the design of the iPad mini that was launched a year earlier .It adopted bezels that were smaller than those on previous models and it was thinner and significantly lighter than its precursors.

Arriving late in 2014 was the iPad Air 2 which was lighter and thinner than the iPad Air before it. This was followed by the release of iPad Air 3 which was released 18 March 2019. The iPad Air 3 took the 10.5 inch iPad Pro as a benchmark for its design, adopting features such as Touch ID home button, a 10.5 inch Retina display and Smart keyboard support.

In September 2020 the 4th generation model the iPad Air, the iPad Air 4 was released. The iPad Air 4 comes with an edge to edge screen of 10.9-inch, Touch Id power button magic keyboard support and an A14 Bionic chip new color variants and more.

FEATURES

DESIGN

Measuring from 10.5 inches to 10.9 inches for the previous iPad Air model, the 2020 Air saw a huge redesign with an edge-to-edge display similar to the iPad Pro screen. The case is aluminum and has flat, rounded edges that surround the Retina display; a design adopted from the iPad Pro. In fact, compared to an 11-inch iPad Pro, the iPad Air is almost indistinguishable except for a slightly thicker body and thicker bezels around the screen.

The iPad Air has a length of 9.74 and a width of 7 inches, while the iPad Pro has its length 9.74 inches and its width 7.02 inches. The iPad Air has a thickness of 6.1 mm while the 11-inch iPad Pro has a thickness of 5.9 mm. The iPad Air weigh 1kg and the iPad Pro weighs 1.04 kg, so there is not much difference here.

Apple's previous iPad Air model has sleek, tapered edges with rounded edges, while the new design has a flatter, more industrial look that matches the iPad Pro and future iPhone 12 models.

This is the first iPad Air with design on all screens and does not have a Home Touch ID button. Face ID is also absent when biometric authentication is performed via the new Touch ID fingerprint reader built into the top button. Touch ID scans a fingerprint like the Home button, but is smaller and more compact. At the top of the iPad Air, next to the Touch ID button, there are speakers and a microphone.

The iPad Air has volume up / down buttons on the right side, a Nano SIM disc in mobile models and a magnetic field to charge the Apple Pencil. There's a single-lens rear camera with a microphone on the back, and a single-lens camera differs significantly from the square camera shot on the iPad Pro because it does not have a second camera or LiDAR Scanner.

The stereo speakers and a USB-C port are located on the bottom of the iPad Air.

COLOUR

The iPad Air's aluminum case is available in five colors and is the first time Apple has offered the iPad in a brighter, unconventional shade. It is Available in Silver, Gray, Gold, Pink, Green or Light-Blue.

Three more available color variants- sky blue pink gold and green - further differentiate the 2020 iPad Air from the 2020 iPad Pro.

DISPLAY

The iPad Air has a 10.9-inch Liquid Retina display, which is the same as the iPad Pro display, but lacks 120 Hz ProMotion technology for a smoother scrolling experience.

It has a resolution of 2360 x 1640 at 246 pixels per inch and a total of 3.8 million pixels. It has full lamination (which reduces the screen thickness and makes the content look more impressive), P3 wide color support for rich, true colors, anti-reflective coating with 1.8% reflectance, 500 nits brightness and True Tone support.

True Tone adjusts the white balance of the screen to match the ambient light to make it easier for the screen to drain the eyes. For example, if you are in a room with more yellow lighting, the iPad screen is warmer, so there is no strong contrast between the color of the iPad and the lighting in the room.

CAMERA

While the iPad Air doesn't have a TrueDepth camera system that supports Face ID, there is an f / 2.0 7-megapixel front-facing FaceTime HD Camera for selfies and video calls.

On the back of the iPad Air is a single-lens 12-megapixel wide-angle camera, which is the same wide-angle camera used on the iPad Pro. It supports higher resolution video and 4K video capture compared to the old iPad Air.

The 12-megapixel camera features all modern improvements such as Live Photos with stabilization, Autofocus with Focus Pixels, wide color capture, exposure control, as well as f / 1.8 aperture for solid low-light performance, Smart HDR, automatic image stabilization, noise reduction and more.

4K video recording such as 120 or 240 frames per second slow motion video is supported at 20, 30 or 60 frames per second. The iPad Air can also record at 1080p at 30 or 60 frames per second, and supports continuous autofocus, cinematic video stabilization, and the option to take 8-megapixel stills while recording 4K video.

A14 BIONIC CHIP

Apple employed the newest 5-nanometer chip technology in the iPad Air 4 with the tablet equipped with the A14 Bionic 6-core chip.

According to Apple, the A14 chip is equipped with 11.8 billion transistors, resulting in higher efficiency and power efficiency. The 6-core design of the A14 chip provides a 40% increase in GPU performance compared to the A12, and the new 4-core GPU architecture provides a 30% improvement in graphics capabilities compared to the A12.

NEURAL ENGINE

The A14 Bionic includes a 16-core Neural Engine that is twice as fast and can handle up to 11 trillion transactions per second with machine learning capabilities faster than ever. The CPU is equipped with second-generation machine learning accelerators that makes machine learning calculations 10 times faster.

With updated GPUs and A14 chips with Neural Engine, Apple says the new iPad will offer powerful new experiences in the device for image recognition, natural language learning, motion analysis and more.

PENCIL SUPPORT

Apple's latest iPad Air is working with the second-generation pencil, which was originally released with the iPad Pro in 2018.Until the release of the iPad Air, the second-generation Apple Pencil was limited to iPad Pro models.

MAGIC KEYBOARD AND TRACK PAD SUPPORT

Like the iPad Pro, the iPad Air is designed to work with the Magic Keyboard, which was released in early 2020. The Magic Keyboard is a folio-style case with a full backlit keyboard and track pad for the first time.

The Magic Keyboard uses scissor mechanisms that are very similar to the MacBook Air and MacBook Pro keyboard. The scissor mechanism provides 1mm of travel, as Apple says it's the best typing experience ever on the iPad.

The Magic Keyboard connects to the iPad Air via a magnetic connection and features cantilever hinges that work on a table or round. The hinges allow the viewing angle to be adjusted up to 130 degrees, so that it can be better adjusted for each use case. The design of the Magic Keyboard allows the iPad to "float" in the air and when used in keyboard mode, the bottom of the case tilts backwards.

The folio-style design of the keyboard covers the front and back of the device, keeping the iPad Air safe when not in use. A USB-C port has been added to the Magic Keyboard for the ability to switch between inductive USB-C charging, leaving the iPad Air's built-in USB-C port free for accessories such as external drives and monitors.

TOUCH ID

IPad Air is the first iPad or iPhone with Touch ID that is not built into the Home button of the device. Apple has included Touch ID on the top button of the iPad Air, allowing biometric authentication based on Touch ID without the need for a thick bezel to occupy the screen.

The top Touch ID button works like the Touch ID Home button and can be used to unlock the iPad Air 4, access apps, shop with Apple Pay and more. The Touch ID on the iPad Air 4 is functional in both portrait and landscape orientation.

USB TYPE C

The iPad Air is the second iPad after the iPad Pro to be updated with the USB-C port instead of the Lightning port. With the USB-C port, the iPad Air can connect to 4K or 5K monitors, cameras and other USB-C devices. The USB-C port supports 5 Gbps data transfer and can charge an iPhone or Apple Watch with the correct cable.

SMART CONNECTOR

The Smart connector on the back of the iPad Air allows it to communicate and power on accessories such as the Magic Keyboard. The Smart Connector interface can transfer power and data, so accessories connected to the iPad Air using the Smart Connector do not require batteries.

BATTERY

The iPad Air is equipped with a 28.6-watt-hour polymer lithium battery, which Apple says will last up to 10 hours while surfing the Internet or watching videos over Wi-Fi. Models with cellular connection take up to nine hours to browse the web. The iPad Air can be charged using the included 20W USB-C power adapter and the USB-C to USB-C cable.

OTHER FEATURES

STORAGE

The iPad Air 4 comes with 2 storage options 64GB and 256GB. It comes with a 6GB RAM.

Wi-Fi 6 and Bluetooth support

The 2020 iPad Air supports Wi-Fi 6, also known as 802.11ax. The updated standard offers higher speeds, improved network capacity, better power efficiency, lower latency and increased connectivity when there are multiple Wi-Fi devices in the same area.

Wi-Fi 6 devices also support WPA3, a security protocol that offers enhanced encryption power. It also supports Bluetooth 5.0.

SENSOR

In addition to a Touch ID sensor, the iPad Air features a three-axis gyroscope, accelerometer, barometer and ambient light sensor for True Tone and other features.

MICROPHONE AND SPEAKERS

IPad Air has two series of speakers for stereo sound in vertical and horizontal mode. Dual microphones for calling, video recording and recording are included.

GIGABIT LTE

The Gigabit LTE class is available on iPad Air mobile models and the LTE modem chip is similar to the chip found on the iPad Pro.

Support for zones 1, 2, 3, 4, 5, 7, 8, 11, 12, 13, 14, 17, 18, 19, 20, 21, 25, 26, 29, 30, 34, 38, 39, 40, 41, 46, 48, 66 and 71 are included.

SIM

There are two SIM options on the iPad Air: a physical Nano SIM slot on the side of the device and a digital SIM designed to work without the need for an eSIM or physical SIM card.

The physical Nano-SIM connector supports Apple SIM, allowing users to switch between carriers seamlessly.

THE iPad AIR 4

SETTING UP YOUR IPAD AIR 4

You can set up your new iPad Air 4 over the internet or by connecting it to your computer. You can also transfer data from other devices such as your iPad, iPhone, iPod touch, or your Android device into your new iPad Air 4.

HOW TO SET UP YOUR IPAD AIR 4

Make sure you have the following.

- A working internet connection either via Wi-Fi or cellular data.

- Your Apple ID couples with your password. If you have none you can create one while during the process of setting up your device.

- You will need your debit card info if you wish to add card to Apple pay.

- Your previous device if you are transferring data to your new device.

Steps to follow

1. Turn on device by holding down the power button until you see the Apple logo come on .If it doesn't come on try charging your device or seeking help from a professional.

2.•Tap on set up manually then simply follow the instructions that come up on the screen.

• If you have iPad touch, iPhone or iPad that has the iPadOS 13 or iOS 11 or higher, you can utilize the quick start option to set up your new device automatically. All you have to do is bring both devices close together and follow the instructions on the screen step by step to copy your preferences, settings, and your iCloud keychain. From your iCloud backup you can then restore other of your data and contents to your new device.

•If your devices run on iOS 12.4, iPadOS 13 or

Thereafter data can be wirelessly transferred to your new device. Keep both devices close to each other both plugged into a power source until the transfer is complete.

•For blind or low vision users simply click thrice on the home button on the side of the iPad Air 4 to switch on voiceover which helps read what's on the screen. You can double tap on the screen with three fingers to enable the zoom in function.

Moving data from your Android device to the iPad Air 4

•If your Android device runs on version 4.0 or later download on PlayStore the move to iOS application.

•On your iPad Air 4 follows the steps below

- follow set up assistant

- When on the app and data screen select move data from Android

•On your Android device

- Turn on Wi-Fi

- launch the move to Android application

- Follow the instructions

SETTING UP CELLULAR SERVICE ON YOUR IPAD AIR 4

Set up cellular plan with e-Sim

1. Open setting and tap on cellular data

2. Carry out one of the following

•To set up a cellular plan, choose a carrier and follow the instructions you see on your screen

•Tap add a new plan to add another cellular plan

•Tap others if you want to scan QR code provided by network carrier or you can choose to input details manually.

You can also download your carrier's app on the Apple store activate your cellular plan through the app and purchase a cellular plan.

INSTALL A Nano-SIM

1. Insert the Sim eject tool into the hole on the outside of the Sim tray and push to eject Sim tray.

2. Take out Sim tray and carefully place Nano- Sim into the tray(observe the orientation to avoid wrong placement of Sim).

3. Insert tray back

4. Provide pin to Sim of you have one set up .

MANAGE CELLULAR DATA SERVICE

Under your settings tap on cellular data and you can do any of the following

1. Put off cellular data and restrict all data to Wi-Fi.

2. Toggle on and off LTE and roaming via cellular data option

3. Put on Hotspot by tapping set up personal Hotspot.

4. Tap manage to manage cellular account

CONNECTING YOUR IPAD AIR 4 TO THE INTERNET

You can do this via cellular network or available Wi-Fi connection.

Connecting to a Wi-Fi connection

1. Navigate to settings and tap on Wi-Fi and then turn on Wi-Fi.

2. To join discovered connections click on the network name and enter password if required

3. Click on others to connect to a hidden network. Input the name, security type and the password of the hidden network.

Look out for the Wi-Fi symbol at the top of the screen to know if your device is connected to a Wi-Fi network.

To join a personal Hotspot
Go to settings and tap on Wi-Fi then select the device name of the device sharing the Hotspot. Input password if required.

Connect to a cellular network
1. Confirm that your SIM is unlocked and activated.

2. Go to settings and tap on cellular data to turn on cellular data connection.

iPadOS14

The main elements of the iPadOS have been redesigned and modernized to take full advantage of the wide canvas the iPad offers. So you can do more, easier than ever.

FEATURES

Redesigned widgets
The View on the iPad Airs widgets has been redesigned to show you more information directly from the Home screen. You can choose from different sizes or add a smart stack of widgets that use intelligence on the device to display the right widget at the right time during the day.

App design
New features such as pull-down menus and sidebars enables you to smartly access functions from your apps all from one location, saving you the hassle of switching views.

Compact calls
Incoming Call notifications from your iPhone, and other third-party apps now come in a new compact display that takes up just a little area of your screen.

Scribble
Scribble enables you use the Apple Pencil as a tool to write in any text field by hand and it gets automatically converted to words.

Automatic conversion
This feature converts handwritten text to typed text automatically.

Write in any text field
The Apple Pencil can be used to write a message or write on your browsers search bar and the handwritten text is converted automatically to typed text . This enables you work on your iPad Air 4 without having to put away the Apple Pencil at regular intervals.

Scratch to delete
This feature enables you delete texts on your iPad air by simply scratching over it with your Apple Pencil.

Circle to select
Simply select words by circling around them .

Notes
With the Apple Pencil, your handwritten notes are captured in a more fluid way.

Smart Selection
Advanced machine learning on the iPad OS enables the iPad Air 4 recognize writing from drawing. With the aid of smart selection you can easily select handwritten texts with the same gestures used for texts that are typed.

Paste handwriting as text
Handwritten notes can be simply select and copied as text which appears as typed text when pasted in another app

Shape recognition
Drawing geometrically perfect arcs, lines and shapes is made easy with shape recognition. The drawing takes an ideal form after a pause at the end of the drawing.

Data detectors
The iPad OS in-built intelligence is able to detect email addresses, phone numbers , addresses and data in handwritten text . Tapping on them gives a list of actions.

Augmented reality (A.R)
Step into the world of A.R and gets a visual feel of the impossible and impractical.

MESSAGES
Added features include;

-Pinned conversation: This enables you keep the 9 most important conversations at the top of your conversation list.

-Group photos: You can now spice up your group conversations by adding a memoji, photo or emoji.

-Inline replies: This enables you direct a reply to a particular message in a group.

-Mentions: You can direct a message to someone by typing the name. Your name is also highlighted when mentioned. Also you have an option of customizing group so that you'll get notifications only when mentioned.

-New memoji and stickers: Pick from over twenty (20) new headwear and hair.

Maps
Using maps to navigate on the iPadOS is easier with features such as cycling direction, Electric vehicle routing and guides .

Safari
Safari offers better performance with the ability to translate website in seven languages. Better passwords monitoring and top notch privacy report to enable you get a good understanding of privacy policies of websites you visit.

Siri
Your favorite virtual assistant comes with a more compact design which lets you access information quickly and help you get things done more efficiently. Siri can now get answers to a larger set of questions using info

from the web. Siri can now also help you send audio messages when you wish to be a lot more expressive.

Application clips
 An application clip is a small part of an application that can be found when you need it. Find application clips by scanning QR codes in Messaging, Maps, and Safari.

SEARCH
 Search is now a unique destination where you can start all your searches. New design and typing experience delivers faster and more relevant results to applications, people and web searches.

Home
Adaptive Lighting allows you to change the lighting temperature throughout the day. Camcorders and bells, you can specify the people you tag in the Photos app and receive notifications when there is traffic in the event zones you have set.

A notification from the home screen on the iPad screen displays an image of a person in the front door with a talk button on the left. Below are accessory buttons for the front door and front lights. Under the accessory buttons, the home address is displayed with the phrase "Ashley rings the bell". There is a Close button in the upper right corner of the alert.

Camera

 Quick video switching allows you to easily change the video resolution and frame rate. A new option in Settings lets you take selfie mirrors that reflect the front camera preview. See Video Capture and take a selfie.

Photos

 Gain access to your albums and search via a sidebar, as well as shared albums and media types. You can easily find photos and videos in Search by adding captions to them. View Photos in Albums, Sort Photos in Albums, and Add Captions and view photo and video details.

Reminders

 Reminders automatically suggest the date, time, and location for a reminder based on similar reminders you've created in the past. You can also assign reminders to people with whom you share lists. See sharing reminders and collaborate.

A Reminders screen displays multiple lists. In the upper left there are smart lists for expiration reminders, scheduled reminders, all reminders and highlighted reminders.

FaceTime

 Participants using sign language can now be detected by FaceTime and tagged in a FaceTime group call. You get even more natural video calls that enable you to make eye contact without staring into the camera.

Privacy

The iPadOS gives you a view of privacy practices of apps on the app store before you downloaded them.

Apps

GETTING APPS ON THE APP STORE FOR YOUR IPAD

Open the app store by tapping on the icon

FINDING APPS

Finding Apps with Siri: give commands like "search the app store for educational apps" or "Get Temple Run game"

You can explore the following options:

-search: you can type in whatever you want and tap search.

-Apps: check out apps that top the chart, newly released apps or explore various categories.

GET INFORMATION ABOUT APPS

The following additional information can be obtained after tapping on an app:

-language supported

-size of app

-compatibility

-family sharing and game center support

-reviews and rating

-In-app pictures

-privacy information

HOW TO BUY AND DOWNLOAD AN APP

1. Tap get if the app is a free app. if you previously bought an app you can download it subsequently without incurring additional charges.

2. Authenticate your Apple ID if required using Face ID, passcode or Touch ID.

USING APP CLIPS

When you find an app clip you can open it in any of the following ways

-Tap on the app cling in Maps, Safari or messenger.

-scan the QR code seen in physical locations such as payment terminals.

DELETING APP CLIPS

Open setting locate apps and them tap on remove all app clips.

APPLE ARCADE SUBSCIPTION

You can subscribe to the Apple arcade on the App store to get access to an awesome collection of games.

You can share your subscription with five family members using family share.

APPLE ARCADE

-You can get access to apple arcade by opening the app store and tapping on Arcade. You can subscribe to the service or manage your subscription.

FONTS

-To get fonts simple go to the App store and download any app containing fonts. Launch the app and install fonts.

-You can manage fonts by going to settings, tap on general and then tap on fonts.

CALENDER

Create and edit appointments, events and meetings using the calendar app.

You can add events by doing the following;

    1. Asking siri by giving commands such as

"Set a meeting "name of person" by "time" "

2. You can also add an event by;

-Tapping on the red plus sign at the top left corner.

-Input the details of the event.

-Tap on add

CREATE AN ALERT

You can create an alert in the following steps;

1. Tap on event and then tap on Edit close to the top right corner.

2. Fill in alert in the event details.

3. Select a time to be reminded.

ADD AND REMOVE AN ATTACHMENT

To add an attachment, while inputting event details, tap on add attachment and select file you wish to attach.

To remove an attachment simply tap an event then tap on edit, swipe over the attachment to the left, then tap on remove.

CAMERA

Take photos on your iPad

You can access your camera by giving a command to Siri to open camera or follow the following steps.

1. Open camera by tapping on the camera icon on your home screen or by swiping left when your phone displays the lock screen interface.

2. Capture a picture by tapping on the shutter button at the bottom or using either of

The volume buttons.

ZOOM IN AND OUT

1. While camera is open pinch the screen with to fingers either inward to zoom out or outward to zoom in.
2. Make use of the slider on the left side of the screen to zoom in or out by siding it either upward or downward.

TAKE PANORAMA PHOTOS

To take a picture in panorama mode take the following steps

1. Select pano mode and tap on the shutter button

2. Slowly move the in the direction indicated by the arrow on the screen while maintaining the center line

3. Tap on the shutter button again to finish.

TO TAKE A SELFIE IN POTRAIT MODE

1. Select portrait mode

2. Align your image with the yellow portrait box.

3. Tap on the shutter or use volume buttons to capture picture.

VIDEO RECORDING

To record a video

1. Open camera by tapping on the camera icon and the select video mode.

2. To start recording tap on the record button or use either volume buttons.

3. While recording pinch on the screen using two fingers to zoom.

4. Tap on the record button to end recording or use either volume buttons.

SCAN QR CODE

Scan QR code using your camera in the following steps

1. Open the camera app and position camera to focus on the QR code.

2. Tap on the notification that comes up on the screen to go to the linked app or website.

CONTACTS

To add new contact tap on the 🔳 sign. You also get suggestions for new contacts from Siri based on other apps you use.

Find a contact

To find a contact tap on the search field located at the top of your contact list. Input a phone number, name or other contact info into the search bar.

Share contact

Tap on the contact you want to share and tap on share contact, then select a method to share the contact info.

Reach a contact

You can select a means of reaching a contact by tapping on any of the buttons below the name of the contact. There is the option to FaceTime the contact, compose email etc.

Delete contact

1. Locate contact's card.

2. Tap on edit.

3. Tap on delete contact.

EDIT CONTACTS

You can add a photo to contact, add birthday, a label and more. Tap on any contact and then tap on edit

-To add photo: simply tap on add photo then select photo or take a new one.

-To add notes: simply on notes field.

-change label: tap on label and select any label on the list or create a custom label of your own.

BASICS

Wake iPad Air 4
Press on the top button or use apple Pencil to touch on the screen

Unlock your iPad Air 4 with face ID
Touch the screen, and then look at your iPad.

-The lock icon moves from the key to unlock to indicate that the iPad is unlocked.

-Swipe up from the bottom of the screen to see the Home screen.

-Press the up button to lock the iPad again. If you do not touch the screen for a minute, the iPad locks automatically.

Unlocking your iPad air 4 using Touch ID

On iPad Air 4, press the up button (Touch ID) using your finger registered in Touch ID.

Tap/ Touch ID button on the top of the iPad.

Press the up button to lock the iPad again. If you do not touch the screen for a minute, the iPad locks automatically.

Unlock using password

-Press the Home button or swipe up from the bottom of the lock screen.

-Enter the password

SWITCH BETWEEN APPS

OPEN APP FROM DOCK
Swipe on the screen from the bottom edge upward while on any app to bring up the dock then tap on any app you want.

USING THE APP SWITCHER
To view all opened apps using the app switcher swipe from the bottom edge of the screen upward. Swipe left or right to view opened app and tap to open the app.

SWITCH BETWEEN APPS
-To switch between apps swipe on the screen left or right with four fingers

-Swipe across the bottom edge of the screen with one finger.

MOVE AND ORGANIZE APPS
To move apps around home page, put them in the Dock or move them to other pages.

-On the home screen touch and hold on any app, and then tap on edit. The apps start to jiggle.

-You can then drag app to another location, the dock at your screens bottom or another home screen page.

-Tap done when you are finished.

TO CREATE A FOLGER AND ORGANISE APPS

Creating a folder on your home screen can help you put a group of apps together so you can easily find them. To create a folder;

-Touch on any app on the home screen and hold down until the apps begin to giggle.

-Drag an app into another to create a folder. You can add other apps to the folder by dragging them into it.

-Tap on the name field if you wish to rename the folder.

-Tap done on the top right corner when you finish.

QUIT AND REOPEN APP

-To quit an app simply open app switcher and swipe the app up to exit.

-to reopen simply locate the app icon and click on it.

DELETE APPS

-To delete apps on your iPad air 4 simple touch and hold on the app to reveal the quick action menu .Tap on delete app the tap on the x sign when the app starts giggling.

-Tap delete then tap done if the apps are still giggling.

You can download deleted apps on the app store.

USING SPLIT VIEW

You can open two apps or open two windows from one app simultaneously using split view to split the screen to accommodate both items separately in different views.

TO open a second item using split view

-while you have an app open simply swipe from the bottom edge of your screen up to bring up the Dock

-Touch, hold and any app you choose from the Dock and them drag it to either the left or right edge of your screen before releasing your finger.

-You can replace an item already open on split view by dragging over the item you wish to replace,

CLOSING SPLIT VIEW

To close split view simply drag app divider against the app you want to close either to the left or right corner of the screen.

SET UP SIRI

To set up siri

-open setting

-search siri

-to activate siri using your voice turn on listen for "Hey siri"

-to activate siri using a button put on Press Home for Siri

ACTIVATE SIRI WITH VOICE

To activate Siri say "Hey Siri" then ask a question or as Siri to perform a task like set a reminder.

ACTIVATE SIRI WITH BUTTON

-press the home button and hold until you hear Siri speak

Siri can be given an array of commands such as

-To search answers to your question from the web.

-Reply a message

-Translate languages

-Play radio station

You can get a list of commands Siri can carry out by saying "Hey Siri" then ask "what can you do"

TURN OFF AND ON YOUR IPAD

-Press and hold on the top button and either of the volume button then wait for the slider to appear then drag the slider up.

-Alternatively you can go to setting, general and then tap on shut down then drag the slider when it comes up.

To turn your iPad Air 4 on press the top button and hold it down until the Apple logo comes up.

FORCE RESTART IPAD

You can force restart your iPad by

- Press quickly on the volume up button and release

-Press quickly on the volume down button and release

-Press on the top button and hold it till the Apple logo comes up then release the button

UPDATE YOUR IPADOS

Update automatically

To update your iPadOS

-Open setting, general and locate software update

-Tap on automatic update and set it to automatically install updates when available.

Update manually

To manually update your iPadOS go to setting, general and tap on software update .On the screen you will see if an update is available.

ACCESSORIES

APPLE PENCIL

PAIR APPLE PENCIL

Place Apple pencil into magnetic connector located at the right side of your iPad.

CHARGING YOUR APPLE PENCIL

-Turn on Bluetooth

-Place Apple pencil into the magnetic connector at the right side of your iPad.

ENTERING TEXT USING THE APPLE PENCIL

Scribble automatically converts text written with the Apple pencil in any field text field into typed texts.

USING APPLE PENCIL TO INPUT TEXT IN NOTE

-Open note and tap on the pencil icon to reveal the markup toolbar

-Tap on the handwriting tool

-Use your Apple pencil to write and it will be automatically converted to typed text.

USING THE APPLE PENCIL TO SELECT AND REVISE TEXT

You can the following using your Apple pencil

-Scratch out text to delete it.

-insert text by touching and holding o an area until a space opens to write on.

-Draw a vertical line between texts to separate or join them.

-TO select a text simply draw a circle around the text or underline it to reveal the editing options.

-To select a word simply use your Apple Pencil to double tap on the word.

-To select a paragraph triple-tap on any word in the paragraph or alternatively drag the apple pencil over the paragraph

TAKE SCREENSHOT WITH THE APPLE PENCIL

-To take a screenshot using you Apple Pencil, from either bottom corner of your iPad swipe up.

-Draw with the apple pencil to mark up screenshot

-Use the markup toolbar located at the bottom of the screen to select drawing tool.

-Tap on the send icon to select sending option.

DRAW AND TAKE NOTES FROM LOCK SCREEN WITH AOOLE PENCIL

While on lock screen tap on Apple Pencil and begin taking notes or drawing.

Apple external keyboards for iPad

Magic Keyboard for iPad

The Magic Keyboard for iPad connects directly to the iPad and closes to create a slim cover (supported models).Includes a built-in trackpad that you can use to browse the iPad screen, open apps and more. The Magic Keyboard for does not make use of batteries or external power

Smart keyboard

The Smart Keyboard connects directly to the iPad and turns into a slim cover. The keyboard does not require batteries or external power.

Magic keyboard

The Magic Keyboard connects to the iPad using Bluetooth. The Magic Keyboard is powered by a built-in rechargeable battery.

Magic keyboard pairing
-Turn on the keyboard.

-Open setting, Bluetooth, and then turn on Bluetooth.

-Tap on the device when it appears under Other Devices list.

Reconnect the Magic Keyboard to the iPad
The Magic Keyboard disconnects when you turn off its switch or move it or the iPad outside of Bluetooth range (approx. 10 meters).

-To reconnect, change the keypad to on or move the keypad and iPad back to the row, and then press any key.

-When the Magic Keyboard is reconnected, the on-screen keyboard does not appear.

Connect the Magic Keyboard for iPad (with built-in trackpad)
You can enter text using the Magic Keyboard for iPad and use the built-in trackpad to control items on the iPad screen.

Install the Magic Keyboard for iPad
-Open the keyboard, fold it again, and then connect the iPad.

-The iPad is magnetically held in place.

-Tilt the iPad as needed to adjust the viewing angle.

Adjust the brightness of the keyboard
Go to Settings> General> Keyboard> Hardware Keyboard, then slide the slider to adjust the dimming level in low light conditions.

Charge your iPad while using the Magic Keyboard for iPad
Plug in the keyboard using the USB-C charging cable and USB-C power adapter that came with your iPad.

Connect the smart keyboard to the iPad
You can use the Smart Keyboard, including the Smart Keyboard Folio, to enter text on the iPad.

To add a smart keyboard, do one of the following:

On iPad with Home button: Connect the keyboard to the smart connection on the side of the iPad.

For other iPad models: Connect the keyboard to the Smart Connector on the back of the iPad.

To use the keyboard, place it in front of your iPad, and then place the iPad in the slot above the number keys.